Meteors

Melissa Stewart

NATIONAL GEOGRAPHIC

Washington, D.C.

For Bruce, who'd like to soar through space
like a meteoroid. —M.S.

The publisher and author gratefully acknowledge the expert review of this book by
Bill Cooke and Danielle Moser of NASA's Marshall Space Flight Center.

Paperback ISBN: 978-1-4263-1943-3
Library edition ISBN: 978-1-4263-1944-0

Book design by YAY! Design

Cover, David Aguilar; 1 (CTR), Walter Pacholka, Astropics/Science Source; 2 (CTR), Tony and Daphne Hallas/Science Source; 4-5 (CTR),
Walter Pacholka, Astropics/Science Source; 6 (CTR), David Aguilar; 7 (LE CTR), Professor25/iStockphoto; 8 (UP CTR), benedek/iStockphoto;
9 (UP CTR), Michael Dunning/Science Source; 10 (LO), Aleksey Kunilov/ZUMA Press/Corbis; 11 (CTR), Billy Kelly; 12, Detlev van Ravenswaay/
Science Photo Library; 13 (LO), Detlev van Ravenswaay/Science Source; 13 (UP), Detlev van Ravenswaay/Science Source; 14 (CTR), Karel-
Gallas/iStockphoto; 15 (CTR), Sinclair Stammers/Science Source; 16-17 (LO), BSIP/Science Source; 19 (CTR), Science Photo Library/Super-
Stock; 20-21 (CTR), Detlev van Ravenswaay/Science Source; 22-23, JPL-Caltech/NASA; 23 (INSET), JPL-Caltech/NASA; 24 (CTR), Alex Cherney,
Terrastro/Science Source; 25 (CTR), David Aguilar; 27, Detlev van Ravenswaay/Science Source; 28-29 (Background), nienora/Shutterstock;
28 (UPLE), NASA; 28 (UPRT), Walter Pacholka, Astropics/Science Source; 28 (LORT), Stephen Alvarez/National Geographic Creative;
28 (LOLE), John Chumack/Science Source; 29 (UP), yurisan/Shutterstock; 29 (CTR LE), David Aguilar; 29 (CTR RT), Tomasz Wyszolmirski/
iStockphoto; 29 (LO), NASA; 30, Manfred Kage/Science Source; 31, NASA; 32-33, NASA; 33 (INSET), O. Louis Mazzatenta/National Geographic Creative; 34, Dan Haar; 35 (UP), Europics/Newscom; 35 (LO), Linda Davidson/The Washington Post/Getty Images; 37, University of
Alabama Museums, Tuscaloosa, Alabama; 38, Emmett Given/NASA; 39 (RT), MSFC/MEO/NASA; 39 (LE), NASA; 40, Emmett Given/NASA;
41 (UP), Thomas J. Abercrombie/National Geographic Creative; 41 (LO), YONHAP/epa/Corbis; 42, powerofforever/iStockphoto; 43, Adolphe
Pierre-Louis/ZUMA Press/Corbis; 44 (UP), stevecoleimages/iStockphoto; 44 (CTR), O. Louis Mazzatenta/National Geographic Creative;
44 (LO), Detlev van Ravenswaay/Science Source; 45 (UP), Thomas Heaton/Science Photo Library/Corbis; 45 (CTR RT), Butsenko Anton/
ITAR-TASS Photo/Corbis; 45 (CTR LE), KarelGallas/iStockphoto; 45 (LO), JPL-Caltech/Cornell/NASA; 46 (UP), David Aguilar; 46 (CTR LE),
Arpad Benedek/iStockphoto; 46 (CTR RT), Cheryl Casey/Shutterstock; 46 (LOLE), Thomas J. Abercrombie/National Geographic Creative;
46 (LORT), Billy Kelly; 47 (CTR LE), Walter Pacholka, Astropics/Science Source; 47 (UPLE), Detlev van Ravenswaay/Science Photo Library/
Corbis; 47 (UPRT), David Aguilar; 47 (CTR RT), Detlev van Ravenswaay/Science Source; 47 (LOLE), PeteDraper/iStockphoto; 47 (LORT), BSIP/
Science Source; header, graphics.vp/Shutterstock; vocab, KamiGami/Shutterstock

National Geographic supports K–12 educators with ELA Common Core Resources.
Visit natgeoed.org/commoncore for more information.

Printed in the United States of America
17/WOR/4

Table of Contents

Streaks of Light

Every day, thousands of small space rocks enter Earth's atmosphere. Together, these meteoroids weigh more than nine buses.

But don't worry. Most space rocks never hit the ground. They burn up as they fall through the atmosphere. And that creates the fiery streaks of light scientists call meteors.

Meteor Meanings

ATMOSPHERE: The layer of gases that surrounds a planet

METEOROID: A small rocky object in space or the atmosphere

METEOR: The streak of light produced as a meteoroid burns up in the atmosphere

If you watch the sky for an hour on a clear night, you will probably see two or three meteors. This time-lapse photo captured six meteors in just eight minutes!

This illustration shows a close-up view of small meteoroids beginning to glow as they enter Earth's atmosphere.

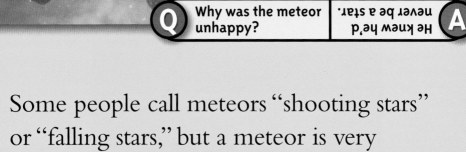

Some people call meteors "shooting stars" or "falling stars," but a meteor is very different from a star.

Most stars are so far away that we could never visit them. They burn bright for billions of years. Most of the meteors we see are about 60 miles away, and their glow lasts just a few seconds.

Most of the meteoroids that enter Earth's atmosphere are smaller than this pea. They burn up long before they reach our planet's surface. But some meteoroids are much larger.

Why do meteors light up the night sky?
Think about it like this: On cold days, you
can warm your hands by rubbing them
together. You create heat because a force
called friction is at work.

★ Meteor
Meaning
FRICTION: A force that resists
the motion between two
objects that are in contact
with one another

Friction can be created in Earth's atmosphere, too. Some meteoroids cruise toward our planet at more than 150,000 miles an hour. As a space rock rubs against gases in the atmosphere, it creates heat. All that heat makes it glow.

Down to Earth

Not all meteoroids burn up completely as they plummet toward Earth. The instant a space rock lands, scientists call it a meteorite. Most meteorites are no bigger than a grain of sand, but some are as big as a boulder.

Meteor Meaning

METEORITE: A space rock that lands on Earth, another planet, or a moon

Around five hundred meteorites land on Earth each year, but only about five of them are ever identified as space rocks.

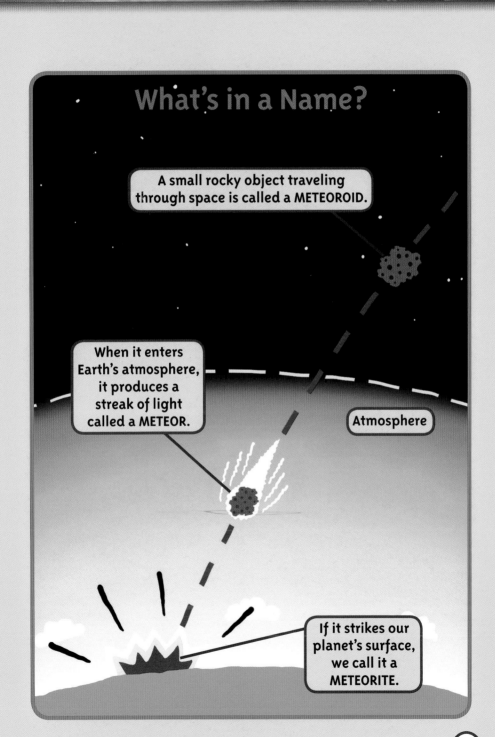

Scientists divide meteorites
into three main groups.

Stony Meteorites

These are the most common
meteorites on Earth, but they're
hard to spot. They look very
similar to Earth rocks.

Some groups of
early peoples
used the iron in
meteorites to
make knife blades.

Iron Meteorites

These meteorites are shiny, so it's easy to tell that they're from out of this world. They're made mostly of two metals—iron and nickel.

Stony-Iron Meteorites

These meteorites are also easy to spot, but they aren't very common. They're chunky mixtures of metal and rock.

Out of This World

Where do meteoroids come from? To find out, you'll need to climb into a space suit and get ready for a long, long journey. We're headed into space.

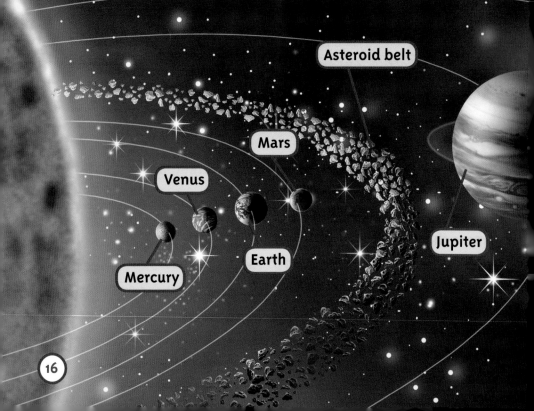

Earth's closest planetary neighbors are Venus and Mars. The asteroid belt, a ring of medium-size rocky objects, orbits the sun between Mars and Jupiter.

Asteroid belt

Mars

Venus

Jupiter

Earth

Mercury

Earth is part of a solar system. The sun is at the center of our solar system, and other objects orbit it.

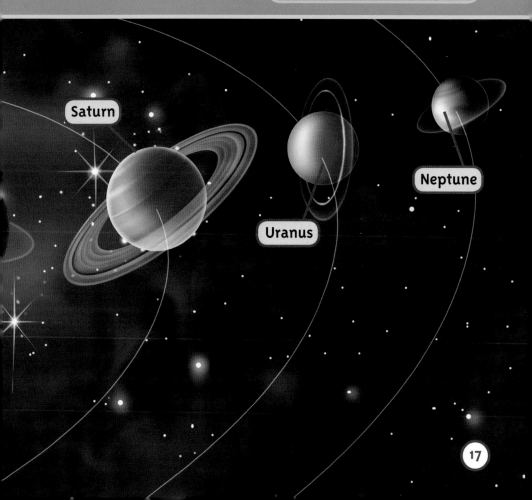

Saturn

Uranus

Neptune

17

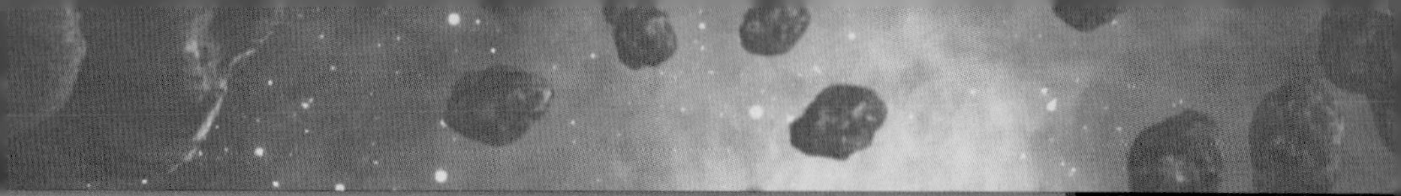

The sun. Some planets.
A bunch of asteroids.
Does our solar system end
there? Not by a long shot!

The planets are surrounded
by a huge area of space
called the Kuiper (KYE-pur)
belt. And that's not all.
A region known as the
scattered disk overlaps part
of the Kuiper belt, and it
stretches far, far out into
space. At the very edge of our
solar system is an even bigger
area called the Oort cloud.

The top part of this illustration shows
a close-up view of the center of our
solar system. The bottom part shows
its position within the Oort cloud.

Q What did the sun say to the Oort cloud?

A You're far out!

Sun

The Kuiper belt is a giant disk that surrounds the planets.

Sun

The Oort cloud is a ball-shaped region at the edges of our solar system. Scientists don't know enough about the scattered disk to draw a picture of it.

Becoming a Meteoroid

The asteroid belt, Kuiper belt, scattered disk, and Oort cloud all contain huge numbers of orbiting objects. At least two million rocky asteroids orbit in the asteroid belt. Many others share an orbit with Jupiter or Mars. The Kuiper belt contains at least a trillion small icy objects, and the Oort cloud may contain as many as two trillion.

An artist's vision of asteroids orbiting in the asteroid belt

Sometimes those orbiting objects break apart, and some of the pieces become meteoroids that eventually enter Earth's atmosphere.

Most objects in space are round, but asteroids come in all kinds of shapes.

Most asteroids speed through space at more than 50,000 miles an hour, so crashes can cause a lot of damage.

From Asteroid to Meteoroid

As asteroids move through space, they crash into each other like bumper cars. Small bits break off and become meteoroids.

Inside an Asteroid

Almost all of the meteorites people find on Earth come from asteroids.

Stony meteorites come from the surface of asteroids.

Iron meteorites come from the core of asteroids.

Stony-iron meteorites come from the area between an asteroid's rocky surface and its metal core.

Most of the time, these new meteoroids stay in the same orbit as the asteroid they came from. But when a meteoroid does get knocked out of its orbit, it may be attracted by the gravity of a nearby planet, such as Earth.

Meteor Meaning

GRAVITY: A force that pulls objects toward the center of a planet or other body

From Comet to Meteoroid

Meteoroids also come from the small objects in the Kuiper belt, scattered disk, and Oort cloud. These objects have rocky cores and icy surfaces. When they get knocked out of these regions and travel toward the sun, they give off gas and dust. Scientists call them comets.

Meteor Meaning

COMET: A chunk of ice, frozen gases, rock, and dust that orbits the sun

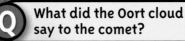

A Comet Up Close

As the sun's gravity pulls a comet toward the center of our solar system, the icy ball heats up and begins to change.

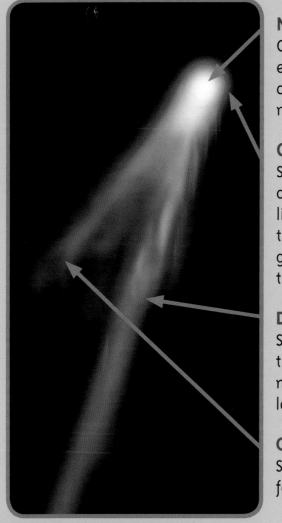

NUCLEUS
Gases and dust escape from the comet's hard, solid nucleus.

COMA
Some gases and dust form a cloud-like coma around the nucleus. They glow brightly as they reflect sunlight.

DUST TAIL
Some of the dust trails out behind the nucleus. It forms a long, thick tail.

GAS TAIL
Some of the gases form a thinner tail.

A comet's nucleus keeps on orbiting the sun, but material from its long dust tail gets left behind. This material becomes tiny meteoroids. Most of the meteoroids that enter Earth's atmosphere come from comets.

As Earth orbits the sun, it follows the same path year after year. And about a dozen times during that journey, it passes through streams of leftover dust from various comets. For a few nights, hundreds of dusty bits enter Earth's atmosphere and burn up. The result is a beautiful display we call a meteor shower.

★ **Meteor Meaning**

METEOR SHOWER: Many meteors coming from the same area of the sky within a short period of time

Meteoroids made of comet dust are so small and fragile that they burn up completely before they hit Earth. This is why we never find meteorites that come from comets.

This illustration shows what you might see over the course of several minutes during a meteor shower.

8 Cool Things About Space Rocks

1 About 12,000 dust-size meteoroids enter Earth's atmosphere each night.

2 Many meteors look orangey red or white to viewers on Earth, but some look green or yellow.

3 A meteor that appears brighter than Venus is called a fireball.

4 Meteorites are usually named after the place where they are found.

5 More meteors can be seen in the hours before sunrise than in the hours after sunset.

6 The meteoroid dust trail left by a comet can be more than 100 million miles long.

7 The rock and metal in most meteorites are about 4.6 billion years old.

8 Bulletproof material helps protect the International Space Station from meteoroids.

Strike Two

Most of the meteorites that land on Earth come directly from asteroids. But asteroids are also the force behind meteorites that come from the moon and Mars.

Meteorites From the Moon

When two asteroids crash, one of them may get knocked out of its orbit. And if its new path crosses the moon's orbit ... *Boom!* Holes called craters mark the spots where asteroids have hit the moon.

During these strikes, bits of the moon fly into space and become meteoroids. Sometimes those rocky bits enter Earth's atmosphere and land on our planet.

Scientists have discovered at least 85 meteorites made of moon rock.

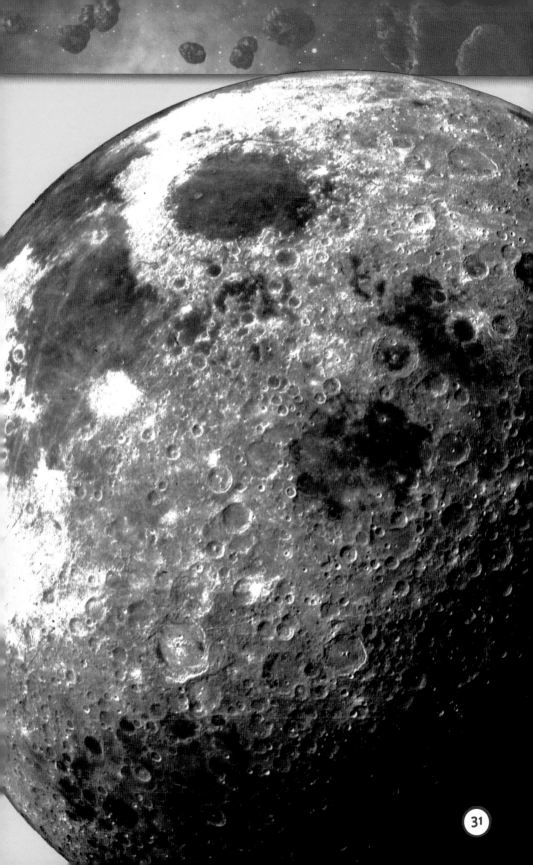

Meteorites From Mars

Like the moon, Mars has been struck by many asteroids. And some of those strikes produced meteoroids.

Some of the meteoroids are still orbiting close to Mars. But others were knocked out of orbit.

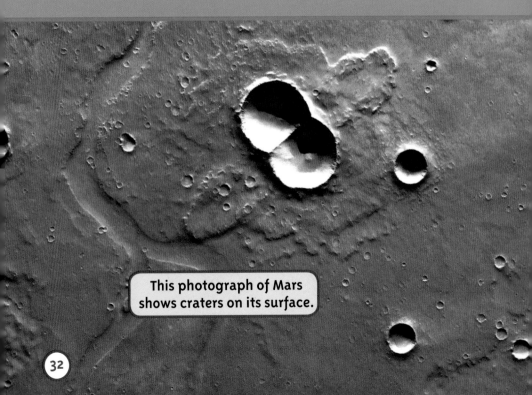

This photograph of Mars shows craters on its surface.

Over time, gravity and other forces moved some Martian meteoroids into Earth's atmosphere. Many of the meteoroids burned up, but a few were large enough to land on Earth as meteorites. So far, scientists have identified 124 meteorites from Mars.

Martian meteorites aren't as easy to find as you might expect. The red rock usually darkens as it travels through Earth's atmosphere.

Struck From Above!

Most of Earth is covered with water, so many meteorites fall into the ocean.

Some land in forests or deserts or other places where people don't live. But once in a while, a meteorite causes damage that people notice.

Wethersfield Meteorite

In 1982, Wanda and Robert Donahue of Wethersfield, Connecticut, U.S.A., heard a strange thud in their living room and rushed to investigate. They couldn't explain the hole in the ceiling until they spotted a grapefruit-size meteorite that had rolled under a piece of furniture.

Peekskill Meteorite

In 1992, Michelle Knapp was startled by a crash outside her home in Peekskill, New York, U.S.A. When she ran outdoors, she discovered that a football-size meteorite had struck her family's car.

Lorton Meteorite

In 2010, a meteorite surprised Dr. Frank Ciampi when it crashed into his office in Lorton, Virginia, U.S.A. The fist-size space rock is now on display at the Smithsonian's National Museum of Natural History in Washington, D.C., U.S.A.

Buildings and cars are fairly large, so it's no surprise that we sometimes hear about meteorites hitting them. But has a space rock ever hit a person? Could a meteorite hit you?

Yes. In fact, maybe one already has. Most meteorites are no bigger than a speck of dust. That means you wouldn't even notice if one plopped down on your head.

What about bigger meteorites? Don't worry. Only about ten people in the whole world have ever been struck by a meteorite large enough that they noticed. And none of them were seriously hurt.

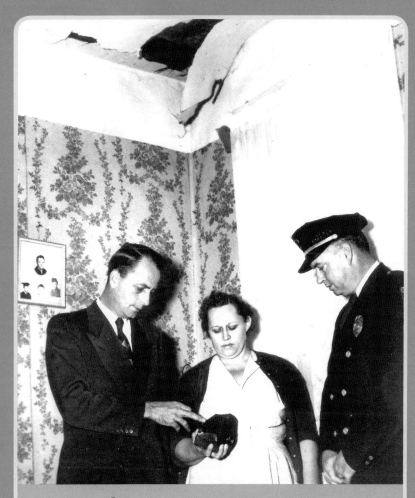

Sylacauga Meteorite

In 1954, a grapefruit-size meteorite smashed through a roof in Sylacauga, Alabama, U.S.A. It bounced off a radio and hit Ann Hodges in the hip while she was taking a nap. She is the only person in the United States who has ever reported being hit by a meteorite.

On the Lookout

Dr. Bill Cooke

Many scientists spend their whole careers studying space rocks. Dr. Bill Cooke, head of NASA's Meteoroid Environment Office in Huntsville, Alabama, U.S.A., tracks meteors as they zip across the night sky.

Cooke uses a network of 12 cameras—
in Ohio, Pennsylvania, Alabama,
Tennessee, Georgia, North Carolina,
and New Mexico—to shoot video
of meteors on clear nights. Then he
determines each meteor's speed, where
it came from, and whether it might have
produced a meteorite. What a cool job!

Cooke's video cameras capture black-and-white images
of meteors. Color is then added to the images (as shown)
to help the details stand out. The image on the left
was created by combining several separate images.

Meteorite Hunt

Other scientists collect meteorites that have landed on the ground. Space rocks can fall anywhere on Earth. But they're easiest to find in two places—hot deserts and frigid Antarctica. Scientists can spot them on the plain tan sand or white ice.

Every year, the National Science Foundation sends teams of scientists to search for meteorites in Antarctica. In the past 30 years, these teams have found more than 16,000 meteorites.

Some "tools of the trade" used by meteorite hunters

This 4,800-pound meteorite was found in the Empty Quarter, a vast desert on the Arabian Peninsula.

A 001

South Korean researchers collected this and other meteorites from a blue ice field in Antarctica in January 2012.

Scientists aren't the only ones who spend time hunting for meteorites. So do lots of other people, including some curious kids.

Would you like to find a meteorite near your home?

Look for a rock that

✓ sticks easily to a magnet

✓ seems heavier than other rocks its size

✓ has a rough surface, indents that look like thumbprints, and/or lots of points and ridges

Many people look for years and never find a space rock, but you might get lucky. You could be the first person in your town to find a meteorite. If you think you've got one, ask the geology department at your local university.

What a Find!

When Jansen Lyons of Rio Rancho, New Mexico, U.S.A., was ten years old, he read a book about meteorites and wanted to find one. After two years of hunting, he came across a rock with all the features of a stony meteorite. Was it really a space rock?

You bet! Jansen's find was later confirmed by Dr. Carl Agee, a meteorite specialist who works at the University of New Mexico's Institute of Meteoritics.

Jansen Lyons found this meteorite near his home when he was 12 years old. Scientists think it fell to Earth about 10,000 years ago.

Be a Quiz Whiz!

How much do you know about meteors, meteoroids, and meteorites? After reading this book, probably a lot! Take this quiz and find out. **Answers are at the bottom of page 45.**

Most meteors are about _____ miles away.
A. 6
B. 60
C. 600
D. 6,000

A meteoroid that lands on Earth is called _____.
A. a meteorite
B. a meteor
C. an asteroid
D. a comet

How many asteroids do scientists think are in the asteroid belt?
A. At least two thousand
B. At least two million
C. At least two billion
D. At least two trillion

4

Most of the meteoroids that enter Earth's atmosphere come from _____.

A. planets
B. comets
C. asteroids
D. moons

5

Most of the meteorites people find on Earth come from _____.

A. Mars
B. the moon
C. asteroids
D. comets

6

A meteorite is usually named after _____.

A. the person who found it
B. the museum where it is displayed
C. the place where it was found
D. the place where it came from

7

A rock could be a meteorite if it _____.

A. sticks easily to a magnet
B. seems heavier than other rocks
C. has a rough surface, indents, and/or lots of points and ridges
D. All of the above

Glossary

ASTEROID: A space rock that's larger than a meteoroid but smaller than a planet

FRICTION: A force that resists the motion between two objects that are in contact with one another

GRAVITY: A force that pulls objects toward the center of a planet or other body

METEORITE: A space rock that lands on Earth, another planet, or a moon

METEOROID: A small rocky object in space or the atmosphere

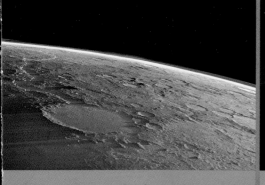

ATMOSPHERE: The layer of gases that surrounds a planet

COMET: A chunk of ice, frozen gases, rock, and dust that orbits the sun

METEOR: The streak of light produced as a meteoroid burns up in the atmosphere

METEOR SHOWER: Many meteors coming from the same area of the sky within a short period of time

ORBIT: To move in a path around another object, such as a star

SOLAR SYSTEM: A star and everything that orbits it

Index